The Gardens of Williamsburg

THIS BOOK on Williamsburg's gardens originated as one of the President's Reports of Colonial Williamsburg. It has been republished in its present form for those who have a general interest in some of the historical background of Williamsburg's gardens and who enjoy photographs of its gardens and greens.

The Gardens of Williamsburg

"...some one always coming to perfection..."

—Thomas Jefferson to Charles Willson Peale 1811

A COLONIAL WILLIAMSBURG PUBLICATION

The Colonial Williamsburg Foundation
WILLIAMSBURG, VIRGINIA

FIFTH PRINTING, 1986
Library of Congress Catalog Card Number: 70-140635
Colonial Williamsburg ISBN: 0-910412-89-8
PRINTED IN THE UNITED STATES OF AMERICA

Two minutes from the heart of town lies the Palace canal, where quiet corners tempt the visitor.

GARDENS have always been one of the primary appeals of Williamsburg. No less an authority than Thomas Jefferson, the last governor of Virginia to live in the Palace, wrote in 1766 from Annapolis to his Williamsburg friend, John Page, that "the houses are in general better than those at Williamsburg, but the gardens are more indifferent."

Mr. Jefferson first visited the colonial capital of Virginia in 1760 to attend the College of William and Mary, and his close association with the city continued until the capital was moved to Richmond in 1780. He greatly admired the beauty of Williamsburg, and the interest he developed here in horticulture and garden design was later expanded at Monticello.

Jefferson's love of growing things never waned, and he gave his attention to gardens–whether flower, kitchen, orchard, or field crop–almost daily throughout a long life. He frequently noted in his garden diary that he had gathered seeds in his travels for planting at Monticello. Some of these came from Williamsburg–a swamp mallow from marshes near the town, and a fine apple tree from the garden of George Wythe's house. The fruit of the tree, he said, was "the most juicy apple I have ever known . . . very refreshing as an eating apple."

In 1811 he wrote the painter, Charles Willson Peale:

> I have often thought that if heaven had given me choice of my position and calling, it should have been on a rich spot

of earth, well watered, and near a good market for the productions of the garden. No occupation is so delightful to me as the culture of the earth, and no culture comparable to that of the garden. Such a variety of subjects, *some one always coming to perfection,* the failure of one thing repaired by the success of another, and instead of one harvest a continued one through the year. Under a total want of demand except for our family table, I am still devoted to the garden. But though an old man, I am but a young gardener.

Jefferson, by the way, is one observer who recorded for us the twin rows of trees that lined Palace Green in his day, as they also do in our own. There is another witness, General Lauberdière of the French army, who described the Palace standing "at the extremity of a handsome street planted with catalpas."

Today, more than two centuries since Jefferson arrived at the college, the presence of the gardens continues to be one of the great joys of Williamsburg. No one who lives here can look about him without catching a glimpse of some green vista, some pattern of shrubbery or flowering tree or borders in bloom. More than one hundred gardens and the broad greens fill ninety of the one hundred seventy-five acres in the Historic Area, and in all seasons and all weathers make the city a sanctuary, a twentieth-century version of the green country town that was an eighteenth-century ideal for some American cities.

When the capital was moved in 1699 from Jamestown to Williamsburg, Governor Francis Nicholson was the major architect for a town plan that remains today a model of artistic and practical accomplishment. The long vistas of the major avenues were enhanced by the broad greens, open spaces which are still so important today in urban planning and renewal programs for our crowded cities.

Soon after Williamsburg became the capital, Francis Michel, a Swiss visitor, wrote in 1701, "Regarding the fruitfulness of the country it may be said that almost everything grows that is put into the ground." The garden settings of Williamsburg endure in today's crowded urban America, and they color the lives of those who live here more than we are aware. There is a year-round sampler of fragrances in Williamsburg's air–the bittersweet of boxwood, the delicate scents of catalpas in bloom along Palace Green, or yellow jessamine or wintersweet, or dozens of other plants and trees. There is an even more impressive year-round display of hue and texture of leaf, trunk, twig, bud, or fruit. It is almost literally true that those of us who live in Williamsburg's Historic Area live in a vast garden.

In many secluded spots our visitors can sense the great variety of the gardens and experience a repose quite rare in our time. Most of our days are pleasant enough for this enjoyment; as William Byrd II wrote, "there are not 10 days in the whole summer that Your Lordship would complain of."

In early summer, when mallard ducklings paddle on the Palace canal, when dogwood, shadbush, and mountain laurel blooms have come and gone and bees are busy over the herbs of the kitchen garden, there is an irresistible urge to sink onto a bench beside the marl path. This canal was once so derided by Virginians as one of Governor Spotswood's extravagances that the governor had the good taste, as well as the means, to offer to pay for it himself. The rush of water over the spillway stills the sound of modern life just beyond the high brick wall, and it is easy to imagine that in more than two and a half centuries of life in Williamsburg, the garden has been at the heart of things.

In this setting one can sense the pleasure with which John Custis, father of Martha Washington's first husband, wrote to a friend in London in 1725: "I have a pretty little garden in which I take more satisfaction than in anything in this world and have a collection of tolerable good flowers and greens from England."

Custis, of course, did not seek escape from a polluted and blighted environment. Instead, perhaps, he sought a sense of order and good husbandry–by contrast a relief from the vast wilderness of this early eighteenth-century continent.

It is Custis, in any event, who has recently added to our knowledge of early Williamsburg gardens. Though we may never know the precise patterns of the plantings made by Custis and his neighbors on the south side of the capital city, we know a great deal about the varieties of plants, how they flourished or perished, those admired by gardeners here and in England, and those propagated by Custis. In a well at the Custis house site, sealed against deterioration since the second half of the eighteenth century, our archaeologists discovered branches and twigs, seeds, and nuts of many plants. Boxwood and holly leaf trimmings, still green after almost two centuries, gave us invaluable evidence about early plant materials in the city. The twenty-one plant species identified in this well were all growing in the Historic Area and substantiate our planting program today.

The ancestry of Williamsburg boxwood may be traced at least as far as 1737, when Custis reported the loss of some "dutch box edgeings" after "the greatest dry season that ever was known in the memory of man." He had two husky gardeners hauling water from his well until nightfall, day after day.

Williamsburg has weathered many crises since that time, and its survival as a small town has made possible its re-created colonial scene. The greatest single asset in the restoration of Williamsburg—with its buildings in a garden setting—lay in the fact that the town had grown hardly at all since the Revolution. Not only were almost one hundred original buildings still standing, but many streets and public greens lay largely undisturbed, and a number of old garden sites had never been built on when the work of restoration began. Market Square in 1926 was a case in point: the Courthouse of 1770 still fulfilled its original function, and cows still grazed on the surrounding green.

Fortunately for us, the "Bodleian Plate," an early eighteenth century copper engraving presented to Mr. John D. Rockefeller, Jr., by the curator of the Bodleian Library at Oxford, England, showed the formal diamond pattern of plantings behind the Palace and the oblong beds in front. Likewise, there was more than a hint of what the Palace gardens were like in Lord Botetourt's inventory, which included "12 Leaden & six stone flower Potts," fragments of which our archaeologists found during excavation of the site. Another striking example

RED MAPLE

GRAPE

The excavation of the John Custis well yielded rich botanical finds—twenty-one species of plants grown here in the eighteenth century. All are growing here today.

ENGLISH HOLLY

HORSE CHESTNUT

PEACH

HONEY LOCUST

DWARF BOXWOOD

AILANTHUS

GOURD

PERSIMMON

LOBLOLLY PINE

SMOKE TREE

RED OAK

NECTARINE

VIBURNUM

VIRGINIA PINE

LINDEN

BLACK WALNUT

SASSAFRAS

CHERRY

HICKORY

of the durability of some garden features was the discovery of the old marl walks at the Palace, giving us precise locations for familiar paths of today. Likewise, the terraces and canal were readily discernible during the research and planning stages of the restoration of the Palace gardens. One of the early developers of the Palace gardens has been identified as Thomas Crease, also gardener of the College of William and Mary. He was once paid for "putting in order the Gardens belonging to the Governor's house."

The results of our restoration program have not only delighted millions of visitors; they have also won the attention of authorities like Peter Coats, who describes the Williamsburg gardens as "imposing and masterly" and includes them in his *Great Gardens of the Western World.*

Behind the beauty of the appealing green vistas all over town lies a comprehensive program of devoted care. More than one hundred gardeners tend the beds, borders, lawns, greens, and wooded areas. I suspect that the public never realizes the full scope of this work.

Fencing, for example, which was first required here by an ordinance of 1704, is one of our concerns. We have more than seven miles of it, picket and board and post and rail in almost infinite variety, most of it kept white by paint crews who never seem to catch up. We have plentiful evidence for the existence of early fences: our archaeologists have found countless postholes for timbers which once supported the pickets and rails that barred livestock from town lots–and kept the animals roaming the streets.

At least once a year our some three thousand trees are given individual attention–feeding, pruning, or major surgery. These trees, especially those lining our streets, were a special concern of Mr. Rockefeller's. He studied them with care, took steps to protect them from damage and disease, and established a nursery for small stock. We are sure that the tradition of a village shaded by majestic trees goes back at least to the close of the eighteenth century. A college student wrote in 1816 that one of his windows "opened into a row of most elegant elm trees whose shade & beauty called forth the most pleasurable ideas." Nathaniel Beverley Tucker wrote in 1844 of "venerable old elm trees of noble growth. . . . They are of the kind commonly called the Dutch elm, and are all probably more than one hundred years old."

Since the beginning of the restoration project we have been able to compile a list of hundreds of native species and imported plants that proved hardy in the Williamsburg area during the colonial and post-colonial periods. Our adherence to the principle of using only plant material proper to the period contributes much, I believe, to the charm of Williamsburg. Through research Colonial Williamsburg continuously seeks new information to make its efforts in this field as authentic as possible.

Mr. Jefferson, most surely, would have a keen interest in our attempts to provide a garden setting for the small city he once knew so well, especially in the use of native Virginia plants. I believe that he would approve the spirit in which we have developed and matured our gardens over about five decades, as a reflection of the colonial love of the green America of two centuries ago.

As Jefferson the gardener once wrote Mrs. Angelica Church in London, in hopes that she might visit Virginia: "I have been planning what I would shew you: a flower here, a tree there; yonder a grove, near it a fountain; on this side a hill, on that a river. Indeed, madam, I know nothing so charming as our own country."

In Williamsburg we hope our gardens will always provide a refuge that will keep that faith.

Carlisle H. Humelsine
President, The Colonial Williamsburg Foundation

The springtime Palace.

Spring comes to Williamsburg with a rush, one day with crocuses in a chilly wind, and the next with dogwood beginning to turn white and the promise of summer in the warm breeze. Abruptly there is a riot of color, and as quickly it has gone.

The tulip show at the Palace.

An unexpected glimpse of the Palace canal.

Species tulips under the pleached beech arbor.

The Palace herb and vegetable garden in peony time.

Typical Williamsburg spring beauty: dogwood, tulips, and greening box at the Roscow Cole House.

Redbud at the Windmill.

The spectacular Benjamin Powell garden, left, at its peak with its Banksia Rose (an introduction of about 1840 favored by a life tenant). Tulips and azaleas are also in flower. Below, the same garden in the peak of dogwood season.

The crisp patterns of formal gardens at the Prentis House complement the lines of fences, roofs, and chimneys, as in this design of clipped yaupon, a native holly once used medicinally by the Indians.

A plum tree sheds its petals over a drowsy garden nook.

A seasonal changing of the guard in tulip time. . . .

White pickets and pink dogwood, a memorable combination.

There are wild gardens, too, where tulips are scattered through native plantings, bees work among quince blossoms, and phlox and mandrakes crowd pine-needle paths. This garden is at the Dr. Barraud House.

Tree peonies in all their glory.

A small formal garden in tulip time.

See my finger vase ↓

The fragrance of Carolina jessamine fills the air.

The Brush-Everard garden house.

A row of leeks comes into bloom.

Summer. There is a drowsiness in the air, and as the sun grows warmer the season matures in slow, sweet days that fade with the last of the crape myrtle.

The summertime Palace.

Hollyhocks frame the Alexander Craig Kitchen.

Walkway companions: ruddy brick, scallop shells, and periwinkle.

Yucca, one of the oldest favorites of all.

Crape myrtle in high summer near Christiana Campbell's Tavern.

The great magnolia of Bruton Parish churchyard.

The first heat of summer in the vegetable gardens at Wetherburn's Tavern.

Broad fields of daylilies.

Blooming chives brighten a doorway.

Flax at harvest time in the field back of the George Wythe House dependencies.

The solitary beauty of the lotus pond endures for weeks.

The bright spires of the native thermopsis.

A shaggy sunflower beside an ancient wall.

Phlox, the long glory of the season.

The noble, luscious fig.

Canada goose on the Palace canal.

A summer shower on Duke of Gloucester Street.

The first tints of autumn touch the Palace gardens and green.

Hawthorn fruits are ripe.

Elms begin to turn and the crops are gathered in at the Ewing House.

Fall lingers in a time of yellowing leaves and chilly nights, when noons are like summer, and the city seems to sparkle with new beauty.

The wind scatters leaves across the George Wythe garden.

An espaliered magnolia clings to a sunny wall—and its cones burst into scarlet.

Dogwood comes to fruit.

The wintertime Palace.

Winter. Snow seldom falls, but when it does, usually drifts softly over our homes and gardens, emphasizing the strength of design in the city's buildings.

Snow touches Duke of Gloucester Street lightly.

A chilly morning fog over a pasture near the Capitol.

A haycock frosted with snow.

The unpredictable patterns of the snow season, like the work of impressionist sculptors.

Late storms sometimes sheathe the city in ice.

Crocuses bring the promise of a new spring.

Dogwood out of season in front of the Pasteur & Galt Little Shop.

The Powder Magazine on the shortest day of the year.

We have over five hundred kinds of cultivated plants in Williamsburg's Historic Area today that were indigenous to Virginia—or were introduced from abroad during the seventeenth, eighteenth, and early nineteenth centuries.

In this volume we have illustrated sixty of these plants that grow in the Historic Area today.

◄
Summer noon—a green country town.

CREDITS

*Photography by N. Jane Iseley, Colonial Williamsburg,
and James L. Amos, National Geographic Magazine.
Design by Richard Stinely, Colonial Williamsburg.
Printed by W. M. Brown & Son, Inc.,
Richmond, Va.*